To My Daughter

with Love

on the
Important Things in Life

To My
Daughter
with Love

on the
Important Things in Life

Susan Polis Schutz

Illustrated by Stephen Schutz

Blue Mountain Press™
Boulder, Colorado

Library of Congress Control Number: 2006027483
ISBN: 978-1-68088-500-2 (previous ISBN: 978-1-59842-172-9)

▐ and Blue Mountain Press are registered in U.S. Patent and Trademark Office.
Certain trademarks are used under license.

Printed in China.
First printing of this edition: 2023

✪ This book is printed on recycled paper.

This book is printed on paper that has been specially produced to be acid free (neutral pH) and contains no groundwood or unbleached pulp. It conforms with the requirements of the American National Standards Institute, Inc., so as to ensure that this book will last and be enjoyed by future generations.

Library of Congress Cataloging-in-Publication Data

Schutz, Susan Polis.
  To my daughter with love : on the important things in life / Susan Polis Schutz ; illustrated by Stephen Schutz. — [New ed.].
      p. cm.
  ISBN-13: 978-1-59842-172-9 (alk. paper) 1. Mothers and daughters—Poetry. 2. Conduct of life—Poetry. I. Schutz, Stephen. II. Title.

  PS3569.C556T6 2007
  811'.54—dc22

                                                                            2006027483

Blue Mountain Arts, Inc.
P.O. Box 4549, Boulder, Colorado 80306

CONTENTS

This book is dedicated and written with a lot of love to my beautiful family.

INTRODUCTION

When To My Daughter with Love on the Important Things in Life was first published in 1985, my daughter, Jordanna, was just a little girl. I never knew what a very special relationship a mother and daughter could have.

As my daughter got older and started to understand more about being female, I felt as if I were once again going through the many stages of growing up. I felt a very strong urge to protect Jordanna from anything that could possibly harm her, but I knew that if I did this, it would hurt her later on because she would not be prepared to face the real world. So instead, I tried to show her and explain to her what I consider to be the important things in life.

Now my daughter has left home and started a wonderful life of her own. The emotions accompanying this passage of time have led me to write new poems, which are included in this new edition of To My Daughter with Love. The poems speak about my philosophy, worries, love, respect, and deepest feelings toward my daughter. These are feelings that most parents have for their cherished daughters.

Though my daughter does not live with us anymore, it doesn't matter where she is, because home is where love and the heart reside.

This book should remind my daughter and all daughters how extraordinarily deep the bond is between parents and their children.

Susan Polis Schutz

"I want you to always know that
in good and in bad times
I will love you
and that no matter what you do
or how you think
or what you say
you can depend on
my support, guidance
friendship and love
every minute of every day"

— Susan Polis Schutz

To My Daughter

My day becomes wonderful
when I see your
pretty face smiling so sweetly
There is such warmth and intelligence
radiating from you
It seems that every day
you grow smarter and more beautiful
and every day
I am more proud of you
As you go through different stages of life
you should be aware that there will be many times
when you will feel scared and confused
but with your strength and values
you will always end up wiser
and you will have grown from your experiences
understanding more about people and life
I have already gone through
these stages
So if you need advice or someone to talk to
to make sense out of it all
I hope that you will talk to me
as I am continually cheering for your happiness
my sweet daughter
and I love you

To My Daughter with Love
on the Important Things in Life

A mother tries to provide her daughter with insight
into the important things in life
in order to make her life
as happy and fulfilling as possible

A mother tries to teach her daughter
to be good, always helpful to other people
to be fair, treating others equally
to have a positive attitude
to make things right when they are wrong
to know herself well
to know what her talents are
to set goals for herself
to not be afraid of working too hard to reach her goals...

(continued)

A mother tries to teach her daughter
to have many interests to pursue
to laugh and have fun every day
to appreciate the beauty of nature
to enter into friendships with good people
to honor their friendships and always be a true friend
to appreciate the importance of the family
and to particularly respect and love our elder members
to use her intelligence at all times
to listen to her emotions
to adhere to her values

A mother tries to teach her daughter
to not be afraid to stick to her beliefs
to not follow the majority when the majority is wrong
to always realize that she is a woman equal to all men
to carefully plan a life for herself
to vigorously follow her chosen path
to enter into a relationship with someone worthy of herself
to love this person unconditionally with her body and mind
to share all that she has learned in life with this person

If I have provided you with an insight
into most of these things
then I have succeeded as a mother
in what I hoped to accomplish in raising you
If some of these things slipped by
while we were all so busy
I have a feeling that you know them anyway
And I certainly hope that you always
     continue to know
how much love and admiration
I have for you
my beautiful daughter

I Love You Every Minute of Every Day,
My Beautiful Daughter

I looked at you today
and saw the same beautiful eyes
that looked at me with love
when you were a baby
I looked at you today
and saw the same beautiful mouth
that made me cry when you first smiled at me
when you were a baby
It was not long ago
that I held you in my arms
long after you fell asleep
and I just kept rocking you
all night long
I looked at you today
and saw my beautiful daughter
no longer a baby
but a beautiful person
with a full range of emotions
feelings, ideas and aspirations
Every day is exciting
as I continue to watch you grow
I want you to always know that
in good and in bad times
I will love you
and that no matter what you do
or how you think
or what you say
you can depend on
my support, guidance
friendship and love
every minute of every day
I love being your mother

I love you so much, my beautiful daughter
I wish that you could see yourself
as others see you —
a sensitive, pretty, loving, intelligent person
who has all the qualities necessary to
become an outstanding woman
Yet sometimes you seem to
have a low opinion of yourself
You compare yourself unfavorably to others
I wish that you would only judge yourself
according to your own standards
and not be so hard
on yourself
I look forward to the day
when you look in the mirror
and for the first time in your life
you see the extraordinary person
that you really are
and you realize how much
you are loved and appreciated
I love you so much
my beautiful daughter
forever as your mother
and friend

I hope that you will have as much confidence in yourself as we have in you.

The True Meaning of Friendship

Some people will be your friend
because of whom you know
Some people will be your friend
because of your position
Some people will be your friend
because of the way you look
Some people will be your friend
because of your possessions
But the only real friends
are the people who will be your friends
because they like you for how you are inside

Try to choose your
friends carefully. Make
sure that they are
worthy of you.

I know that lately you
have been having problems
and I just want you to know
that you can rely on me
for anything
you might need
But more important
keep in mind
that you are very capable
of dealing with any complications
that life has to offer
So
do whatever you must
feel whatever you must
and realize
that we all
grow wiser and
become more sensitive and
are able to enjoy life more
after we go through
hard times

My dear daughter
you have come out of a time
mingled with problems
wiser, happier
and much smarter
I am so proud of the way
you handled yourself
the way you thought out the proper solutions
and the strength you used in following through
I no longer have to worry about you
You are very capable of leading your own life
and I know any decisions
that you make for yourself
will be right
You can't imagine how happy this makes me
You are a wonderful person and
a beautiful daughter
I love you dearly

ove is
being happy for the other person
when that person is happy
being sad for the other person
when that person is sad
being together in good times
and being together in bad times
Love is the source of strength

Love is
being honest with yourself at all times
being honest with the other person at all times
telling, listening, respecting the truth
and never pretending
Love is the source of reality

Love is
an understanding so complete that
you feel as if you are a part
of the other person
accepting that person
just the way he or she is
and not trying to change each other
to be something else
Love is the source of unity

Love is
the freedom to pursue your own desires
while sharing your experiences
with the other person
the growth of one individual alongside of
and together with the growth
of another individual
Love is the source of success

Love is
   the excitement of planning things together
   the excitement of doing things together
Love is the source of the future

Love is
   the fury of the storm
   the calm in the rainbow
Love is the source of passion

Love is
   giving and taking in a daily situation
   being patient with each other's
      needs and desires
Love is the source of sharing

Love is
   knowing that the other person
   will always be with you
      regardless of what happens
   missing the other person when he or she is away
   but remaining near in heart at all times
Love is the source of security

Love is
   the
   source
   of
   life

Love is the most important
emotion that you will ever
have. I hope that you are
able to open yourself up
to a beautiful love. I have
tried to express what love means
to me. You will discover your
own meaning.

Finding the right person to love
is so important
Love comes naturally
but you must both work
at making it last
and try your hardest
at all times
to be fair and honest with each other

Strive for your own goals
and help your mate achieve his
Always try to understand him
Always let him know what you are thinking
Always try to support him
Try to successfully blend
your lives together
with enough freedom
to grow as individuals
Always consider each day you spend together
as a special day
Regardless of what events
occur in your lives
make sure that your
relationship always flourishes
and that you always
love and respect each other

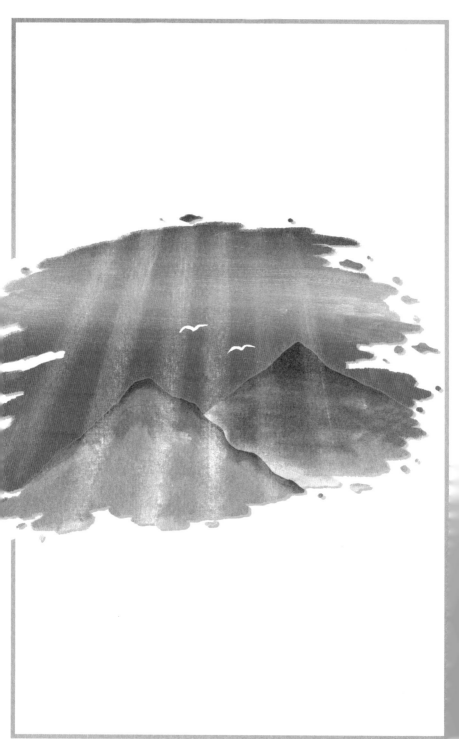

Don't be afraid
to love someone
totally and completely
Love is the most fulfilling
and beautiful feeling in the world
Don't be afraid that you will
get hurt
or that the other person
won't love you
There is a risk in
everything you do
and the rewards
are never so great
as what love can bring
So let yourself get involved
completely and honestly
and enjoy the possibility
that what happens
might be the only real
source of happiness

My darling daughter
I am glad that
you were born in an age
when women
don't always have
to fight so hard to be heard
The world is wide open
for you to be whatever you want
It will be hard
but at least you
will find other women
striving for the same thing
and you won't be called "crazy"
for wanting to achieve your goals
You are living in an age
where womanhood is
finally growing
to be everything
that it can be
My darling daughter
I have watched you play with
dolls and trucks
footballs and toads
and I picture you
my beautiful child
as a beautiful woman
in full control of her life

*I*t is very difficult
for a woman
to have a
successful career and
happy children and an
exciting personal life

When attending to work
most women feel guilty
because they are not with their children
When attending to their children
most women feel guilty
because they have work to do
And if there is time
for personal things
most women feel guilty
because they are neither
attending to the needs of their children
nor their work

In order for a woman
to successfully do
all the things she wants to
she must delegate the things
she does not want to do —
and her husband must equally
share family responsibilities
Otherwise
all the demands on the woman
leave her too tired and frustrated
to enjoy life
And that just isn't fair

Many women
I have talked to lately
tell me that they are
extremely unfulfilled
being housewives
that their work all day
is so unimportant
that they are not using
their minds —
These women must
do something that
interests them
but they must also
be reassured that
being a good mother is an
extremely important job
and that just because society
seems to say that raising children
is a menial task
there is no reason to believe this
In fact many beliefs that society
imposes on the individual
are wrong
Women must realize
that whatever they do
is important
as long as they do it well

A woman will get only what she seeks
Choose your goals carefully
Know what you like
and what you do not like
Be critical about what you can do well
and what you cannot do well
Choose a career or lifestyle that interests you
and work hard to make it a success
but also have fun in what you do
Be honest with people
    and help them if you can
but don't depend on anyone
    to make life easy or happy for you
(only you can do that for yourself)
Be strong and decisive
but remain sensitive
Regard your family, and the idea of family
as the basis for security, support and love
Understand who you are
and what you want in life
before sharing your life with someone
When you are ready to enter a relationship
make sure that the person is worthy of
everything you are physically and mentally
Strive to achieve all that you want
Find happiness in everything you do
Love with your entire being
Love with an uninhibited soul
Make a triumph
of every aspect
of your life

Find happiness in everything you do.

*We cannot
listen to what
others want us
to do
We must listen
to ourselves
We don't need to
copy other people's ways
and we don't need to
act out certain lifestyles
to impress other people
Only we know
and only we can do what
is right for us
So start right now
You will need to
work very hard
You will need to
overcome many obstacles
You will need to go
against the better
judgment of many people
and you will need to
bypass their prejudices
But you can have
whatever you want
if you try hard enough
Start right now so that
you can live a life
designed by you and
for you —
a life you deserve*

*Only you
can choose the
lifestyle you
want to
follow.*

Live Your World of Dreams

ean against a tree
and dream your world of dreams
Work hard at what you like to do
and try to overcome all obstacles
Laugh at your mistakes
and praise yourself for learning from them
Pick some flowers
and appreciate the beauty of nature
Be honest with people
and enjoy the good in them
Don't be afraid to show your emotions
Laughing and crying make you feel better
Love your friends and family with your entire being
They are the most important part of your life
Feel the calmness on a quiet sunny day
and plan what you want to accomplish in life
Find a rainbow
and live your
world of dreams

Always have dreams.
Always try to make
them a reality.

You Are One of Those Rare People
Whose Dreams Will Become a Reality

What makes people succeed
is the fact that they have confidence in themselves
and a very strong sense of purpose
They never have excuses for not doing something
and always try their hardest for perfection
They never consider the idea of failing
and they work extremely hard toward their goals
They know who they are
and they understand their weaknesses
as well as their strong points
They can accept and benefit from criticism
and they know when to defend what they are doing
They are creative people
who are not afraid to be a little different
You are one of these rare people
and it is so exciting to watch you
on your path to success
as you follow your dreams
and make them a reality

I Am Ready to Listen

I suspect that
you are thinking about something
that is bothering you
Please share any problems
that you might be having
with someone (it doesn't matter with whom)
because if you just keep these problems in your mind
you will not be able to pursue
your thoughts and activities
to your fullest potential
nor will you be able to enjoy
all the great things in life
because problems, whether they are large or small
often dominate one's thoughts
You are such a wonderful person
and you should always be happy
and free from nagging worries

I want to remind you that
I am always ready to
listen to you in an understanding way
so if you ever need me
I am always here for you

*S*ometimes I talk to you
and I am not really sure
what you are thinking
It is so important
to let your feelings
be known
Talk to someone
Write your feelings down
Create something based on your feelings
but do not keep them inside
Never be afraid to
be honest with people
and certainly never be afraid to
be honest with yourself
You are such an
interesting, sensitive, intelligent person
who has so much to share
I want you to know
that wherever you go
or whatever you do
or whatever you think
you can always depend
on me, your mother
for complete and absolute
understanding
support
and love
forever

lder people
could teach us
so much
if we would
only listen
Their wisdom
their simplicity
their experiences
their many years of living
We need them to
live with us
with our families
to teach us
and our children
all they know
to love us
and to let us
love them
and to let us
help them
when they
need it
A family
is not complete
without its
eldest
members

The love
of a family
is so
uplifting

The warmth
of a family
is so
comforting

The support
of a family
is so
reassuring

The attitude
of a family
toward
each other
molds one's
attitude forever
toward the
world

I Want You to Live a Life of Love, My Daughter

We brought you into this world
a beautiful little girl
born of love
who would one day
grow up to be
a beautiful woman full of love

I tried to teach you
important values and morals
I tried to show you
how to be strong and honest, gentle and sensitive
I tried to explain to you
the importance of achieving your own goals
I tried to express
the need to reach out to people
I tried to emphasize
the beauty of nature
I tried to demonstrate
the extreme importance of family
And I tried, every day, to set an example
that you could look up to

When we brought you into the world
I did not think about how everything
could be destroyed in a few minutes
in a world not at peace
in a world with nuclear weapons

I taught you love
in a sometimes hateful world
because it is love that can abolish hate
before hate abolishes us

I am very sorry, my beautiful daughter
that these destructive forces
have been handed down to you
All of the mothers
and all of the fathers
in the entire world
must unite together and
dedicate ourselves to
ending violence as a way
of solving problems
We must do this so that we can assure you
my daughter, and all children
that you will grow up
to hike in the mountains
and run in the fields of flowers
so that we can assure you
that you will have a chance to grow up
to live a life
of peace and
love

You are a shining
example of what a
daughter can be —
loving and compassionate
honest and principled
determined and independent
sensitive and intelligent
You are a shining
example of what every
mother wishes her
daughter were
and I
am so very
proud of
you

f you know yourself well
and have developed a sense
of confidence in yourself
If you are honest with yourself
and honest with others
If you follow your heart
and adhere to your own truths
you are ready to share yourself
you are ready to set goals
you are ready to find happiness
And the more you love
and the more you give
and the more you feel
the more you will receive
from love
and the more you will receive
from life

The freer you are
with your emotions
and feelings, the more you
will be able to give and
receive love.

Sometimes you
think that you
need to be perfect
that you cannot
make mistakes
At these times
you put so much
pressure on yourself
I wish that you
would realize
that you are
like everyone else —
capable of
reaching great potential
but not capable of
being perfect
So please
just do your best
and realize that
this is enough
Don't compare yourself
to anyone
Be happy to be
the wonderful
unique, very special
person that you are

*A friend is
someone who is concerned
with everything you do*

*A friend is
someone who is concerned
with everything you think*

*A friend is
someone to call upon
during good times*

*A friend is
someone to call upon
during bad times*

*A friend is
someone who understands
whatever you do*

*A friend is
someone who tells you the truth
about yourself*

*A friend is
someone who knows
what you are going through at all times*

*A friend is
someone who refuses to listen
to gossip about you*

A friend is
someone who supports you
at all times

A friend is
someone who does not
compete with you

A friend is
someone who is genuinely happy for you
when things go well

A friend is
someone who tries to cheer you up
when things don't go well

A friend is
an extension of yourself
without which
you are not complete

Everyone needs people to
understand them throughout
life. I hope that you have at least
one good friend for life. I
have tried to define what a
friend is to me...

I Am Always Here for You

Since you were born
you have been
such a beautiful
addition to our family
Now that you are growing up
I can see that
you are a beautiful
addition to the world
As I watch you
doing things on your own
I know you will find
happiness and success
because I am confident in
your ability
your self-knowledge
your values
But if you ever need a boost
or just someone to talk to
about difficulties that
might be occurring
I am always here
to help you
to understand you
to support you
and to love you

I Love Your Beautiful Smile, My Daughter

Sometimes I see you
confused
Sometimes I see you
troubled
Sometimes I see you
hurt
and I feel so sad and
helpless
I wish that I could absorb
these feelings from you
and make everything better
but I know that these feelings
will only help you to grow
and understand more about life
These feelings will help you
to become a more sensitive person
So as I watch your eyes
which tell me everything
I will offer you my
understanding and support
I will offer you my
love
I will offer you the
promise that your beautiful
smile will soon return

My daughter
when you were born
I held you in my arms
and just kept smiling at you
You always smiled back
your big eyes wide open
full of love
You were such an
angelic
good
sweet baby
Now
as I watch you grow up
and become your own person
I look at you
your laughter
your happiness
your simplicity
your beauty
and I wonder where you will be
in fifteen years
And I know that you will
be able to enjoy a life
of sensitivity
goodness
accomplishment
and love
I want to tell you that
I am so proud of you
and I dearly
love you

What Is a Daughter?

 daughter is
a rainbow bubble
a star glimmering in the sky
a rosebud after a storm
a caterpillar turning into a butterfly

A daughter is
hair flying in the wind
red cheeks that glisten in the sunshine
big daydream eyes

A daughter is
a wonder
a sweetness, a secret, an artist
a perception, a delight

You are all these things
and so much more
You are everything that is beautiful

To My Daughter, I Love You

So many times
   you ask me questions
    and your big beautiful eyes
    look at me
    with trust, confusion and
   innocence
I hope that my
answers to you
will help guide you
Even though I always want to protect you
and step in for you when you have a
   difficult decision to make
it is very important that I do not interfere
so that you will learn from your own experiences
and develop confidence in your own judgment
There is a fine line between
a mother telling her daughter
too much
or too little
I hope I have struck a proper balance
I have always wanted to tell you
how honored I am that you
seek out my opinions
I appreciate the trust you have in me and
I want you to know that
I have an immense trust in you
I am very proud of you and
I love you

Ever since you were born
you have been a bundle of
perpetual motion
Your energy is endless
Your mind is unbounded
You want to touch, smell, feel and do everything
You want to live life to the fullest
But don't forget
you are extraordinarily creative
and it is hard for creativity to flourish
unless there is a certain amount
of quietness and peace
So you will, at times, need to quell
your vigor
stop your movements
and let the perpetual motion of your mind
leap to new bounds
as you bask in the stillness of your
spirit and soul

*ou have continually
demonstrated your
incredible intelligence, creativity
and ability to work very hard
Your accomplishments
have soared*

*You have risen
to heights
way beyond your years
I am so proud of you
Your noble morals —
despite the way of the world
Your strength —
while many people are weak
And your sensitivity —
when many people are uncaring
You are a very special individual
because you are able to
stick so firmly to your principles
I think you have discovered
who you are, however —
I want to be sure that
you are in touch
with your heart and emotions
as well as your intellect
so that you will be
able to develop the kinds
of close relationships that
together with your accomplishments
will make you truly happy*

Your soft sensitive side
will need to blend with your
worldly side
And you will need to learn to
ignore the mean words of others
as well as their excessive praises
You, not other people
must be the judge of your life
And in the future
I hope you can spend
more time being free
to do what you want
You are a very creative spirit
who needs to fly more
I love the
respect and friendship that
we have discovered
with each other
It is so much fun
talking and going places
with you
We have a lot in common —
often seeing things
no one else notices
smelling things
no one else smells
observing and understanding people's obscure
peculiarities and characteristics
I enjoy being with you, Princess
and I love you

I remember so well
when you were eleven months old and
you jumped over your high crib wall
and happily ran to my room
delighted in your newfound freedom
I remember so well
your soft bouncy hair
falling over your huge inquisitive eyes
your little rosebud lips quietly
chuckling at things you found funny
and your sunny red cheeks
against your porcelain baby face
Though it seems so long ago
you are the same now
only taller and older
Your hair still
falls over your enormous eyes —
eyes that twinkle with
intelligence and innocence
Your little rosebud lips speak
with big sophisticated words and ideas
and often chuckle in a cynical way
at things you find funny
Your cheeks are red from
outdoor sports
and your skin is still
so soft and delicate

And now
your quest for independence
that began in your crib
is taking on new dimensions every day
as you experiment to find your way
You always work so hard
to do your best
while giving your entire mind and heart
to the new avenues you try
I proudly observe your journey
and I know that wherever it leads you
you will have outstanding successes
and you will have fun, happiness and challenges
because in your search
you will discover
your own
reason for work
significance for your heart
and meaning for your life

My Daughter,
I Am So Proud of You

Every day
I am astounded
to hear you talk
   so intelligently
Your wisdom grows
   and grows
as you do
You are such a delight
such a joy
such a beautiful person
The love I see
   in your eyes for me
is so moving and rewarding
And I hope you
   see and feel
the infinite love I have for you
Whatever you do
wherever you go
know that
I am always here
in every way
for you

ool
as the melting snow
as the summer breeze
as the mist rising from the fog
Cool as the cliché was intended

Cool
as you go places for fun
as you pursue whatever you desire
as you don't care what people think
as you can do things alone
as you are spontaneous
Cool as you can be carefree

My daughter... "so cool"
Cool attitude
Cool independence
Cool actions
Cool life

ou are such an outstanding person
and I hope nothing ever changes
your inner beauty
As you keep growing
remember always
to look at things the way you do now —
with sensitivity
honesty
compassion
and a touch of innocence
Remember that people and situations
may not always be
as they appear
but if you remain true to yourself
things will be all right
With your outlook, you will see
the good in everything
and this will reflect back to you
When I look ahead
I see happiness for you on every level
and I am so glad
because that is what every mother
wishes for her daughter

I often marvel at your strength
to not give in to current misguided
morals and trends
I look at others your age —
some going through life aimlessly
and I know your journey
must be tough and lonely
because it is hard to be an individual
in a world of followers
where it is easy to go along with the crowd
It is so important for people
to actually choose the way to conduct their lives
And because you have done this
your relationships and accomplishments
will be genuinely deserved
and though there may not be a lot of people
with whom you will feel a kindred spirit
the people you find who are similar to yourself
will be the ones
who stand apart from the crowd
They, like you
will make a difference
in the world
with their dreams and actions

You are so modest
that you really don't know or believe
how you are viewed by others
and in a way, that is nice
People respect and admire you
They see you as being extremely
intelligent and knowledgeable
strong and tenacious
creative and innovative
sensitive and kind
moral and honorable
fair and pretty
fun-loving and witty
athletic and vigorous
They see you as
a leader
a thinker
a doer
I think you possess all of
these attributes and more
and you don't even know it
which keeps you unassuming
and in a way, that is nice
Words cannot express
how proud I am of you
Only my heart can show you
how much I love you

To My Wonderful Daughter

To see you happy —
laughing and dancing
smiling and content
striving toward goals of your own
accomplishing what you set out to do
having fun alone and with your friends
capable of loving and being loved
is what I have always wished for you

Today I thought about your beautiful face
and felt your excitement for life
and your genuine happiness
and I am so proud of you as I realize that
my dreams for you have come true
What an extraordinary person you are
and as you continue to grow
please remember always
how very much
I love you

Daughter...

*When you need someone
to talk to
I hope you will
talk to me*

*When you need someone
to laugh with
I hope you will
laugh with me*

*When you need someone
to advise you
I hope you will
turn to me*

*When you need someone
to help you
I hope you will
let me help you*

*I cherish and love
everything about you —
my beautiful daughter
And I will always support you
as a mother, as a person
and as a friend*

We Will Be with You Always

This is your last year at home
then to college
new people
new environment
new learning
I know you are
more than ready
to absorb the dazzling knowledge
from the ivory towers
of lofty minds
but are you ready
to leave the familiar
surroundings of your
loving home and
small-town environment?
Don't be afraid
You are so strong
in your beliefs and values that
you will be comfortable
in any situation in which
you find yourself
because you will be in charge —
choosing the best aspects
and avoiding the worst
You are ready, Honey —
Your mind needs new challenges
Your soul needs new like souls
And always remember that
though we will say good-bye for now
your family deeply loves you
Wherever you are
we will be right there with you —
in your dorm, in the library, everywhere you are —
in our minds and in our hearts
I love you

e a part of as many things as possible
Soak up everything
Look everywhere
Feed your spirit
Feel different emotions
Be extremely curious
Think differently than what is expected
Touch nature
Search humanism
Now is NOT the time to limit possibilities
Now IS the time to experiment
Now IS the time to learn and grow
Now IS the time to explore
life's potential

ou are so
precious to me
I love everything about you
If you are having a problem
I wish I were the one
having it and
I also wish I could
help you
If you are confused about
something difficult
just try to think about it
without barriers

My love for you
includes all difficulties
you will ever have
So remember
I am supporting you
and loving you
always

don't feel different
but I look at you —
and how you have changed
from a baby to a young woman
and I must be different also
Years and years have passed
as I watched you grow up
and I grew up alongside you
and loved you
more each day

*A*re you strong enough to counter
any problems that occur
naysayers who tell you that you can't
disappointments that leave you frustrated
stinging words of others that hurt your feelings
obstacles in your path that make you want to quit
relationships that are sad or unhealthy

And are you strong enough to enjoy
the beautiful aspects of life
people who encourage you
friends who really care about you
kind and complimentary words of others
highlights on your individual path that are exciting
relationships that are worthwhile and deep
literature, music and art
solitude and nature
and your own
independence and happiness

Yes, Dear, though you may not feel it at times, you are strong enough.

Daughter, I Know That
Your Dreams Will Come True

You are a unique person
and only you can do whatever
it takes to follow your dreams

So let your spirit lead you
on a path of excitement
and fulfillment
And know that
because you are a
determined, hardworking
talented and independent thinker
your dreams can
become realities

hen you have problems
unless you tell me
I cannot help
I cannot even offer you my support
When you lived at home
you didn't have to talk
because I'd see problems in your eyes
So I worry more now
because troubled eyes enter my sight
and I can't even kiss your cheek
so you can feel my support

*M*y daughter
I want to thank you
for being
the fine, sensitive, beautiful
person that you are
and extra thanks
for being
so easy to raise
You have made it
so easy for me
to be a parent
I will always love you

My Promise to You, My Daughter...
I Will Always Care About You and Your Happiness

want you to have a life of happiness
In order for you to have this
you must have many interests
and pursue them
You must have many goals
and work toward them
You must like your work
and always try to get better
You must consider yourself a success
by being proud of doing your best
You must have fun
You must listen to your own voice
You must have peace
and not always expect perfection
You must have respect
for yourself and others
My daughter, as I watch you grow up
I can see you are on the right path

My Beautiful Daughter

f ever things are not
going well for you
and you have some problems to solve
If ever you are feeling confused
and don't know the right thing to do
If ever you are feeling frightened
and hurt
or if you just need someone
to talk to
please remember that
I am always here for you
ready to listen
without passing judgment
but with understanding
and love

My little daughter
(but no longer little)
As you grow into a young adult —
a bouquet of exquisite, vigorous flowers
and I look at you with awe

Drink enough water of life
so you passionately blossom
When it is dark and cloudy
know that light will soon
shine through a clear sky

Absorb enough sunshine
to keep you warm
Absorb enough wind to flood you
with free-flowing movements

My young adult daughter
(but no longer little)
The fragrance of your world
will guide you
And I look at you with love

This Is for Those Times When You Just
Need to Know That Someone Cares

Sometimes we do not feel
like we want to feel
Sometimes we do not achieve
what we want to achieve
Sometimes things happen
that do not make sense
Sometimes life leads us in directions
that are beyond our control
It is at these times, most of all
that we need someone
who will quietly understand us
and be there to support us

I want you to know
that I am here for you
in every way
and remember that though
things may be difficult now
tomorrow is a new day

If You Want to Turn
Your Dreams into Reality...

Do what you love
Control your own life
Have imaginative, realistic dreams
Work hard
Make mistakes but learn from them
Believe in yourself but know your limitations
Ignore people who tell you that you can't
Plow through obstacles and failures
Try to turn your dreams into reality

About the Author and Artist

Susan Polis Schutz is an accomplished writer, poet, committed feminist, and documentary filmmaker. She began her writing career at the age of seven, producing a neighborhood newspaper for her friends in the small country town of Peekskill, New York, where she was raised. Upon entering her teen years, she began writing poetry as a means of understanding her feelings. She continued her writing while attending Rider University, where she majored in English and biology and later received an honorary doctor of laws degree. Following her graduation from Rider, she entered a graduate program in physiology, while at the same time teaching elementary school in Harlem and contributing freelance articles to newspapers and magazines. Today, she is the author of many best-selling books of poetry illustrated by her husband, Stephen Schutz, including To My Daughter with Love on the Important Things in Life, which has sold over 1.8 million copies. Her poems have been published on over 450 million books and greeting cards worldwide.

Susan's latest undertaking is creating documentary films that make a difference in people's lives with her production company, IronZeal Films™. Anyone and Everyone, her very first film released in 2007 for which she was both executive producer and director, featured the coming-out stories of gay sons and daughters and their parents. It was, in part, inspired by Susan's own son, Jared Polis, Colorado's first openly gay governor. From there, Susan has gone on to explore a number of other important topics in such films as Seeds of Resiliency, Following Dreams, Over 90 & Loving It, The Misunderstood Epidemic: Depression, It's "Just" Anxiety, and The Homeless Chorus Speaks.

Her latest documentary, Love wins over hate (October 2020), explores the lives of six former white supremacists and ultraconservatives. Each tells of their transformation from being filled with hate, anger, and rage to acceptance and appreciation of diversity. They talk honestly and openly about their former beliefs, the pain they have inflicted on others, and their fight for a better world devoid of hate. All of Susan's films have been broadcast to great acclaim on PBS stations throughout the country. Susan's films can be viewed on the Susan Polis Schutz YouTube channel, youtube.com/ironzealfilms.

As a thriving poet, entrepreneur, activist, and best-selling author, Susan is not only a teacher but also a student of life... who seeks the truth and shares the lessons with the world. To learn more about Susan's latest endeavors, you can visit her Facebook page.

Stephen Schutz is an avid conservationist as well as an accomplished artist, photographer, and calligrapher. A native New Yorker, he spent his early years studying drawing and lettering as a student at the High School of Music and Art in New York City. He went on to attend MIT, where he received his undergraduate degree in physics. During this time, he continued to pursue his great interest in art by taking classes at the Boston Museum of Fine Art. He later entered Princeton University where he earned his PhD in theoretical physics. In addition to designing and illustrating all of Susan's books, Stephen is the genius behind bluemountain.com — the internet greeting card service he created and cofounded with the help of his and Susan's elder son, Jared — which became one of the most popular and widely visited websites in the world. He holds a patent for his 5-D™ Stereograms, which are innovative, computer-generated illustrations and photographs containing hidden, multidimensional images that seem to "come alive."

Stephen also founded Starfall.com, an interactive website where children have fun learning to read and do math. Starfall is used by millions of students in almost every school in the United States and other countries, and each year they complete over a billion educational activities. In 2015, the Polis-Schutz family donated Starfall to the Starfall Education Foundation, a nonprofit organization, after supporting the project as a social enterprise for fifteen years.

Together, Susan and Stephen are the cofounders of Blue Mountain Arts, the internationally renowned publisher known for its distinctive greeting cards, gifts, and poetry books. In her 2004 autobiography, Blue Mountain: Turning Dreams Into Reality, Susan recounts how she and Stephen met in 1965 at a social event at Princeton. Together, they participated in peace movements and antiwar demonstrations to voice their strong feelings against war and destruction of any kind. They motorcycled around the farmlands of New Jersey and spent many hours outdoors with each other enjoying their deep love and appreciation of nature. They daydreamed of how life should be.

In 1969, Susan and Stephen married and moved to Colorado to begin life together in the mountains where Susan did freelance writing at home and Stephen researched solar energy in a laboratory. On the weekends, they experimented with printing Susan's poems, paired with Stephen's paintings, on posters that they silk-screened in their basement. They loved being together so much that it did not take long for them to begin disliking the nine-to-five weekday separation that resulted from their pursuing different careers. They decided that their being together all the time was more important than anything else. So Stephen left his research position in the physics laboratory, and he and Susan set out in their pickup-truck camper to spend a year traveling across the country and selling their silk-screened posters in towns and cities along the way. Their love of life and each other, which they so warmly communicate, touched people everywhere they went, and in response to incredible public demand for more of the couple's unique and inspiring creations, their first book, Come Into the Mountains, Dear Friend, was published in 1972.

Of all their tremendous accomplishments, Susan and Stephen agree that their most fulfilling life experience has been being parents to their three children and grandparents to their two grandchildren. After fifty-four years of marriage, they are more committed than ever to each other, to their family, and to inspiring people to greater heights through film, art, poetry, and education. Theirs is an atmosphere of joy, love, and spontaneous creativity as they continue to produce the words, the poems, the rhythm, and the art that have reached around the world, opening the hearts and enriching the lives of more than 500 million people in every country, in every language, in every culture. Truly, our world is a happier place because of this perfectly matched and beautifully blended couple, Susan Polis Schutz and Stephen Schutz.

Stephen Schutz and Susan Polis Schutz   Photo by Rocky Thies

Stephen Schutz and Susan Polis Schutz   Photo by Stephen Schutz

Jordanna